Do You Really Want to Drive in a Blizzard?

A Book about Predicting Weather

ROAD CLOSED

ADVENTURES IN
SCIENCE
ADVENTURES IN

WRITTEN BY DANIEL D. MAURER · ILLUSTRATED BY TERESA ALBERINI

AMICUS ILLUSTRATED
is published by Amicus
P.O. Box 1329, Mankato, MN 56002
www.amicuspublishing.us

Paperback edition printed by RiverStream Publishing in arrangement with Amicus.
ISBN 978-1-62243-359-9 (paperback)

Library of Congress Cataloging-in-Publication Data
Names: Maurer, Daniel D., 1971- author. | Alberini, Teresa, illustrator.
Title: Do you really want to drive in a blizzard? : a book about predicting
weather / written by Daniel D. Maurer ; illustrated by Teresa Alberini.
Description: Mankato, Minnesota : Amicus, [2017] | Series: Amicus illustrated
| Series: Adventures in science | Audience: K to grade 3. | Includes
bibliographical references and index.
Identifiers: LCCN 2015040671 (print) | LCCN 2015041049 (ebook) | ISBN
9781607539599 (library binding : alk. paper) | ISBN 9781681510712 (eBook)
Subjects: LCSH: Weather forecasting—Juvenile literature. |
Blizzards—Juvenile literature.
Classification: LCC QC995 .M38 2017 (print) | LCC QC995 (ebook) | DDC 551.63—dc23
LC record available at http://lccn.loc.gov/2015040671

Editor: Rebecca Glaser
Designer: Kathleen Petelinsek

Printed in the United States of America at
Corporate Graphics in North Mankato, Minnesota.

HC 10 9 8 7 6 5 4 3 2 1
PB 10 9 8 7 6 5 4 3 2 1

ABOUT THE AUTHOR

Daniel D. Maurer writes for both children and adults and
lives in Saint Paul, Minnesota with his wife, two boys,
two cats, and one dog. They all dig science together.
Visit *www.danthestoryman.com* to learn more.

ABOUT THE ILLUSTRATOR

Teresa Alberini has always loved painting and drawing.
She attended the Academy of Fine Arts in Florence,
Italy, and she now lives and works as an illustrator in a
small town on the Italian coast. Visit her on the web at
www.teresaalberini.com.

You've been planning to visit your cousins up north for weeks. But it's snowing, and the weather could get worse. Do you really want to drive in a blizzard?

Driving in a blizzard isn't safe. The weather forecast predicts 3 inches (7.6 cm) of snow and high winds. That could create a blizzard. But it's not storming yet, so you take a chance.

Will the weather forecasters be right? Predicting weather is tricky, because it can change so fast. How do they do it?

First they collect data. Weather stations all around the world measure air temperature and wind speed. They record rainfall and snowfall. They also measure barometric pressure, or how much air is pressing down on the earth. When the pressure is low, it often creates stormy weather. When it's high, there is mostly sunny weather.

Meteorologists compare the data to past weather. They look for patterns. And they create weather models. The models use a lot of high-level math to calculate weather predictions. All the data goes to a supercomputer that runs the calculations.

Sometimes the predictions are wrong. But today, the forecasters were right. The wind has picked up—a lot.

The light snow you started driving in has turned into a blizzard. You can see only about $^{1}/_{4}$ mile (0.4 km). You'll have to get off the road.

Meteorologists also look at radar. Radar shows how big and fast storms are and which direction they're going. This blizzard is blowing to the east—it will hit the next town in about an hour.

After you call your cousins to tell them you'll be late, your phone rings.

"Hi Grandma! We're stopped at a truck stop because of a blizzard. What's the weather like in Florida?"

"It's sunny and nice, dear."

Why is the weather so different?

Geography affects the weather quite a bit. Florida is much farther south than your home, and Florida is right by the ocean. The wind blows over the warm waters and warms the air. In Florida, it's often 70°F (21°C), even in winter.

17

But people in Florida need weather forecasters, too. Why?
Hurricanes. These storms form over warm ocean water. Clouds
start to spin around an area of low pressure called the "eye."

A hurricane brings lots of rain and wind
and can rip apart homes. You want to be
prepared if one is coming!

Wherever you live, meteorologists will study and predict the weather to keep people safe.

And look, the blizzard finally blew past. Plows have cleared the road. Now you can get to your cousins' house safely!

A barometer measures air pressure. Make one to use at home and see how the air pressure changes over time.

MAKE YOUR OWN BAROMETER

WHAT YOU NEED:

- Large empty glass jar
- Drinking straw
- Balloon
- Rubber band
- Tape
- Paper
- Pencil

WHAT YOU DO:

1. Blow up the balloon and release the air to stretch out the rubber.
2. Cut off the "neck" of the balloon and throw it away. Keep the large round section.
3. Stretch the round balloon piece over the jar. Place a rubber band around it so the balloon stays tight.
4. Tape the drinking straw to the center of the balloon stretched over the jar.
5. Tape the paper to a wall. Slide the jar so the edge of the straw is 1/2 inch (1.3 cm) from the paper. Mark with the pencil where it currently points.
6. High air pressure will press down on the balloon and make the straw point up. Low air pressure lets the balloon rise, and makes the straw point down.
7. Look outside. What's the weather during low pressure? What's the weather during high pressure?

In this book, you learned that meteorologists measure data to predict the weather. Collect some data of your own and try predicting the weather yourself!

WHAT YOU NEED:

- Notebook
- Pen or pencil
- Outdoor thermometer
- Barometer (or Internet site with local weather stations)

DAY OBSERVATION	MONDAY	TUESDAY	WEDNESDAY	THURSDAY	FRIDAY	SATURDAY	SUNDAY
TEMPERATURE MORNING							
TEMPERATURE AFTERNOON							
TEMPERATURE EVENING							
PRESSURE MORNING							
PRESSURE AFTERNOON							
PRESSURE EVENING							
WEATHER PATTERN CHANGE?							

WHAT YOU DO:

1. Pick three times during the day you will be able to measure the weather data and make observations.
2. In your notebook, make a chart. Put the days of the week across the top. On the left, make a column listing temperature and barometric pressure for each time you chose.
3. At the times you've chosen, check the thermometer and record the temperature.
4. Then check the barometer and write down the number it shows.
5. Write down what the weather is like—sunny, cloudy, windy, rainy, or stormy for example.
6. At the end of the week, look for patterns in your data. What happens to the temperature during the day? How does the barometric pressure seem to affect the weather? What do you think the weather will be like next week?

GLOSSARY

barometric pressure—A measurement of how much the air in the atmosphere pushes down on the earth.

blizzard—A bad snowstorm in which wind speed is over 35 mph (56 km/h) and snow prevents you from seeing past ¼ mile (0.4 km) for at least three hours.

data—Facts and measurements that are recorded; weather data includes temperature, wind speed, barometric pressure, and precipitation.

forecaster—Someone who uses data and studies patterns to predict what will happen in the future.

hurricane—A rotating storm with winds at least 74 mph (119 km/h) and often heavy rain. Hurricanes can be very dangerous and destructive.

meteorologist—A person who studies the atmosphere, weather, and climate. They also forecast the weather.

radar—An electronic device that sends out short pulses and receives waves that bounce back; these waves tell the location of rain or snow.

READ MORE

Boothroyd, Jennifer. **How Does Weather Change?** Minneapolis: Lerner Publications Company, 2015.

Furgang, Kathy. **National Geographic Kids Everything Weather: Facts, Photos, and Fun that Will Blow You Away.** Washington D.C.: National Geographic, 2012.

Schuetz, Kristin. **Severe Weather**. Minneapolis: Bellwether Media, 2016.

WEBSITES

SciJinks: All About Weather
http://scijinks.jpl.nasa.gov/
Find answers to your weather questions.

University of Illinois Extension: Tree House Weather Kids
http://extension.illinois.edu/treehouse/index.cfm
Read more about temperature, air pressure, and other weather terms or choose a fun activity.

Weather Wiz Kids
http://www.weatherwizkids.com
Meteorologist Crystal Wicker explains predicting weather, extreme storms, and more, just for kids.